Animals and their Ancestors

Written by Tess Schembri
Series Consultant: Linda Hoyt

WorldWise™
Content-based Learning

T0360023

Contents

Introduction

Long, long ago, the first animals on Earth lived in the oceans. Over time, the oceans changed. Slowly, the animals that lived in the oceans also changed. Their bodies changed, their behaviour changed and their life cycles changed so they could survive in their new environment.

water environment

transitional period

385 million years ago

375 million years ag

Over millions of years, some animals adapted in ways that enabled them to leave the ocean. They developed features that made it possible for them to live on land. They could breathe air. They grew limbs and could travel away from the ocean to find food. Many animal **species** developed.

Since then, animals have continued to change, sometimes adapting to new environments. Some change is slow, but with a few animal species, change has been amazingly fast.

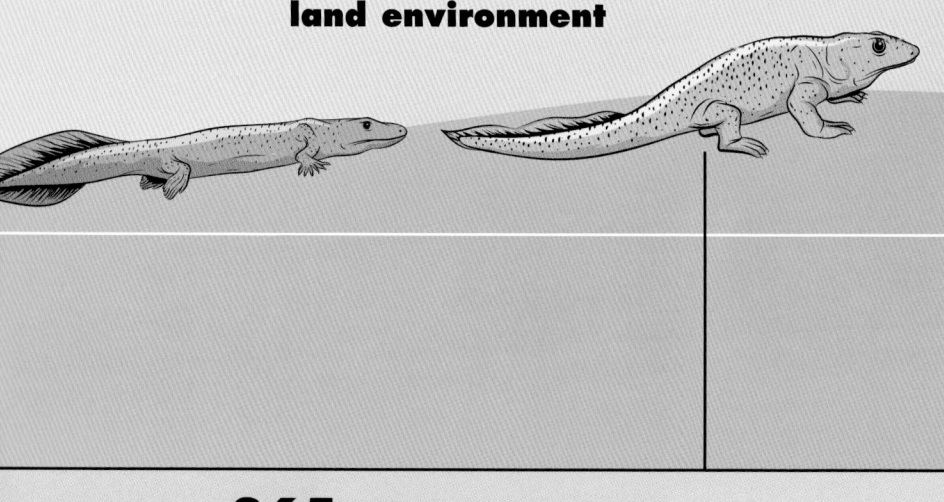

land environment

365 million years ago

Scientists have discovered **fossils** that show fish developing into amphibians and moving out of the water and onto the land. It took millions of years for these changes to happen.

Chapter 1

Changing slowly

Most animal **species** change slowly. For some animal species, scientists have found many **fossils** that show how the species has changed over time into the animal we know today.

Common ancestors

The whale and the hippo have the same **ancestor**. What does this mean?

Both animals are mammals. Their common **ancestor** was a four-legged water-loving animal that lived many millions of years ago and belonged to a group of animals with hooves. Scientists know this from studying the fossil remains of these animals.

Over millions of years, as the environment changed, two new animal species developed from this one **ancient** animal.

One eventually developed into the animal that became the modern hippopotamus. The other developed into the species of animal that became whales, dolphins and porpoises.

Early ancestor — *Pakicetus*

Whale

Hippo

The grey whale lives in the ocean and eats tiny shrimp-like animals. This animal does not have teeth. It has brush-like plates in its mouth that filter food from the seawater.

The hippopotamus lives on land, but it spends most of its day in fresh-water. At night, it comes out of the water onto the land and eats large amounts of grasses and other plants. It has huge tusk-like teeth.

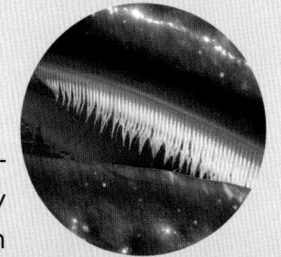

Close-up of brush-like plates in a grey whale's mouth

Close-up of hippo teeth

Horses

Scientists have an excellent fossil record for the horse. The ancestor of the modern horse was the size of a small dog. It did not have hooves. Instead, it had four toes on its front legs and three on its back legs. It grazed on fruits and leaves.

Over 50 million years, the small animal slowly changed into a huge animal. Now, the modern horse has very different teeth, which enable it to eat grass. It has just one toe, which is a hoof, on each leg and much stronger bones in its front legs.

Horses and their ancestors

An ancestor is the living thing that a species originated from. Find out more about the ancestors of horses in North America. Have they always lived there?

The evolution of the horse

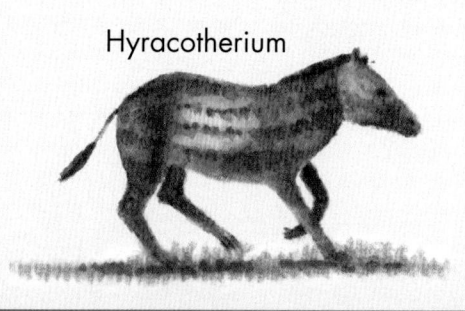

Hyracotherium

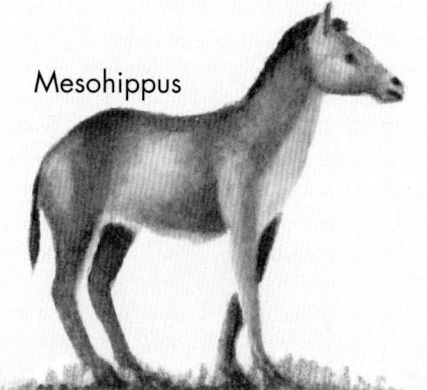

Mesohippus

60 million years ago   **40 million years ago**

Merychippus

Equus

30 million years ago   **10 million years ago**

Birds

Did you know that modern birds developed from small meat-eating dinosaurs?

Scientists think that the ancestor of the modern bird was a small dinosaur. This dinosaur had a long tail, teeth and feathers. As well as being able to fly, it walked on land and perched like a bird. Some of these dinosaurs also built nests to lay their eggs in and kept their eggs warm.

The ability to fly eventually allowed these dinosaurs to travel further in search of food and to live where no other animals could go. This gave them advantages over other animals, such as access to food and safe breeding grounds.

An artist's impression of the flying dinosaur archaeopteryx.

Archaeopteryx fossil from 150 million years ago

Pelicans

African grey parrot

Great horned owl

Over millions of years, the bodies and behaviours of these animals slowly changed into the thousands of bird species we have today.

Each species lives in its own **habitat** for feeding, sometimes migrating for nesting and breeding. Over time, the bodies of birds became lighter. The chest muscles of flying birds grew much bigger so they could move their wings faster or for longer periods. Some developed feathers that helped them fly better or feathers that allowed them to survive in the coldest places.

Scientists believe that modern birds are all related to archaeopteryx, a small flying dinosaur.

A Galápagos finch

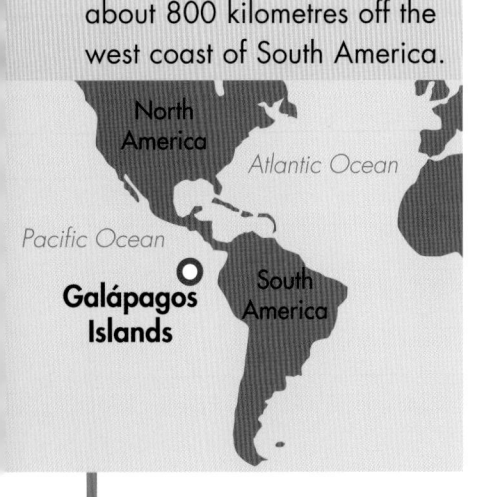

The Galápagos Islands are about 800 kilometres off the west coast of South America.

Modern finches

The Galápagos Islands in the Pacific Ocean are far from land. The animals that live there are isolated because the islands are so far away from any other land.

The scientist Charles Darwin visited the Galápagos Islands over two hundred years ago. He noticed that the small birds that lived on these islands had different body sizes, beak shapes, feeding behaviours and songs. Their different beaks allowed them to eat different foods such as insects, nectar, and seeds.

All these small birds were finches, and they all had a common ancestor. Over time, the finches had adapted to eat different diets so they did not all **compete** for the same food.

Finches that live on the Galápagos Islands

Small ground finch

Seeds

Cactus ground finch

Cactus fruits and flowers

Vegetarian finch

Buds

Woodpecker finch

Insects

Chapter 2

Living fossils – staying the same

Today, some animals look very much the same as they did millions of years ago. They have survived changes in their environment without having to change.

Why? Because they haven't had to change. Even though their environment changed, they were still able to find the things they needed to survive.

Platypuses like this one haven't changed much from their ancestors. Fossils more than 100 million years old show the animals are similar.

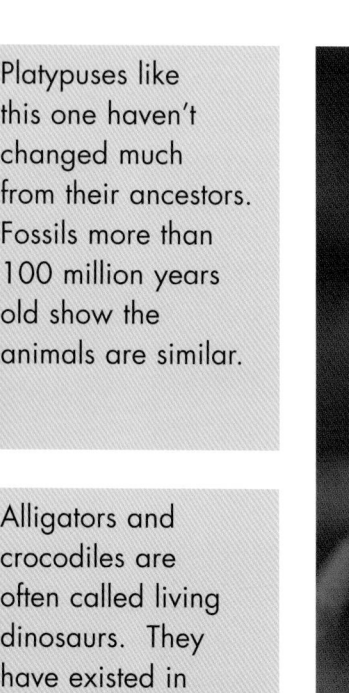

Alligators and crocodiles are often called living dinosaurs. They have existed in their current form for about 80 million years.

The North American opossum has changed very little over the past tens of millions of years.

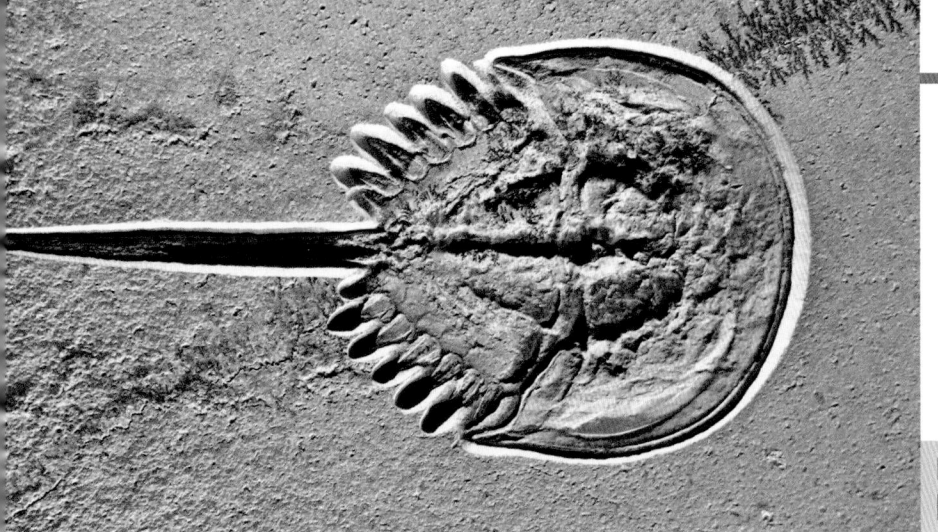

Fossil of a
horseshoe crab

A living
horseshoe crab

Horseshoe crab

The body of the horseshoe crab has changed very little over
400 million years. **Fossils** of horseshoe crabs show what they
looked like millions of years ago. It has the same body shape
as that of horseshoe crabs today.

Horseshoe crabs live in shallow ocean waters in many
parts of the world. Sometimes they come ashore to
mate. They feed mainly on worms and sea snails and
sometimes on small fish.

A nautilus swimming in the sea

Nautilus

The fossil of a nautilus

The nautilus is an animal that is found in tropical waters in the Pacific and Indian oceans. This animal belongs to the same group of animals as snails, which are **molluscs**. The nautilus has a soft body and lives in a shell. It eats shrimp, crabs and fish, and scavenges on any dead animals.

Scientists have discovered fossils of nautilus **species** that are 500 million years old. These fossils look very much the same as the modern nautilus.

Tuatara

These reptiles are found on small islands off the coast of New Zealand, where they have no predators.

At night, they prey on beetles and other insects, spiders, birds' eggs and small reptiles. Tuataras live in burrows that are sometimes shared with seabirds. These animals look much the same as their **ancestors** of 200 million years ago.

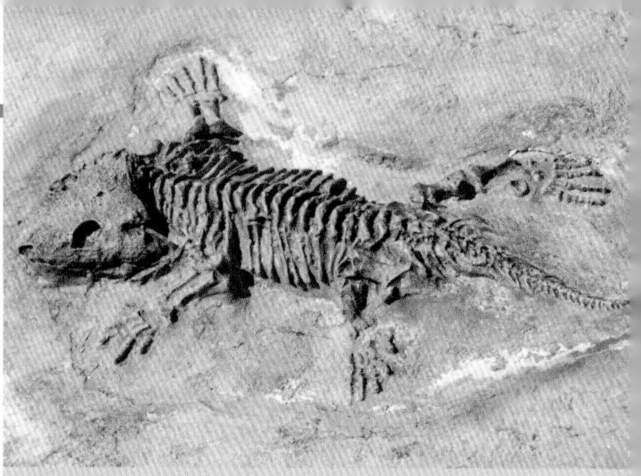

Above: the **fossil** of a tuatara.
Below: a tuatara

17

Chapter 3

Changing quickly

We can understand the process of how animals change by looking at changes to animal bodies and behaviour that have taken place over a much shorter period.

Florida green lizard

Florida, in the United States, has a native green lizard that is often seen there and in nearby states. This lizard changed when a similar brown lizard was introduced from Cuba.

Both the green and brown lizards eat the same food. They hunt beetles, spiders and other small insects and animals that live on the ground. The brown lizards were larger and heavier than the green lizards. They were better at hunting for food.

The green lizards were not getting enough food on the ground. They were forced up into the trees to hunt for food. The food in the treetops is mostly flying insects that are harder to catch, but the green lizards were able to catch enough food to survive.

The green lizard developed larger toes and pads to help it climb trees.

Scientists compared green lizards on islands where there are no brown lizards with green lizards that have moved into trees. They found that the lizards that live in trees had developed toes that give them better grip in the treetops where they live and hunt. The green lizards with the better grip have survived, and those without have disappeared.

The green lizards were forced into a new environment and have changed and adapted to their new **habitat**. These changes happened in just over 15 years.

This shows how quickly an animal can change and adapt.

Did you know?

Scientists have discovered that the green lizards that live in trees have these special features on their toes to help them climb trees:
- larger toe pads on their longest fourth toe
- more sticky scales on their toe pads.

The Florida green lizard

The Florida brown lizard

Tawny owl

Tawny owls are found in the forests of Europe. They come in two colours – pale grey or brown.

In winter, when it snows in the cooler parts of Europe such as Finland, the grey owl blends into the snowy environment. It is safe from predators because it is hard for them to see it.

But scientists have observed that the number of grey tawny owls in Finland has dropped in the past 30 years, and the number of brown owls has increased. This is because the climate is changing. Winters in Finland are not as cold, and the snow cover season is shorter.

Now, there are more brown owls because their brown feathers help them blend in with the brown bark on trees.

As more brown owls survive, they breed and produce even more brown owls. The grey owls are at risk of disappearing.

Owls inherit their feather colour from their parents. With more and more brown owls breeding, the **gene** for grey feathers is less common.

Find out more

Tawny owls nest in tree trunks. How could the cutting down of forests threaten the tawny owl population? Do you think the tawny owl would be able to adapt to this sort of change? How might it do this?

21

Chapter 4

Human intervention

Changes in some species of animals are caused by the direct action of humans. The pets in our homes and the animals on farms today are all quite different from their ancestors. They have been changed by the actions of humans.

The ancestors of dogs were wild wolves. Some of these wolves lived near humans. During times when people moved from place to place hunting their food, wolves have fed on the bones and remains of animals that the people discarded.

Some wolves became tamer or less frightened of humans and people found them useful for hunting or guarding their camps.

When were farm animals domesticated?

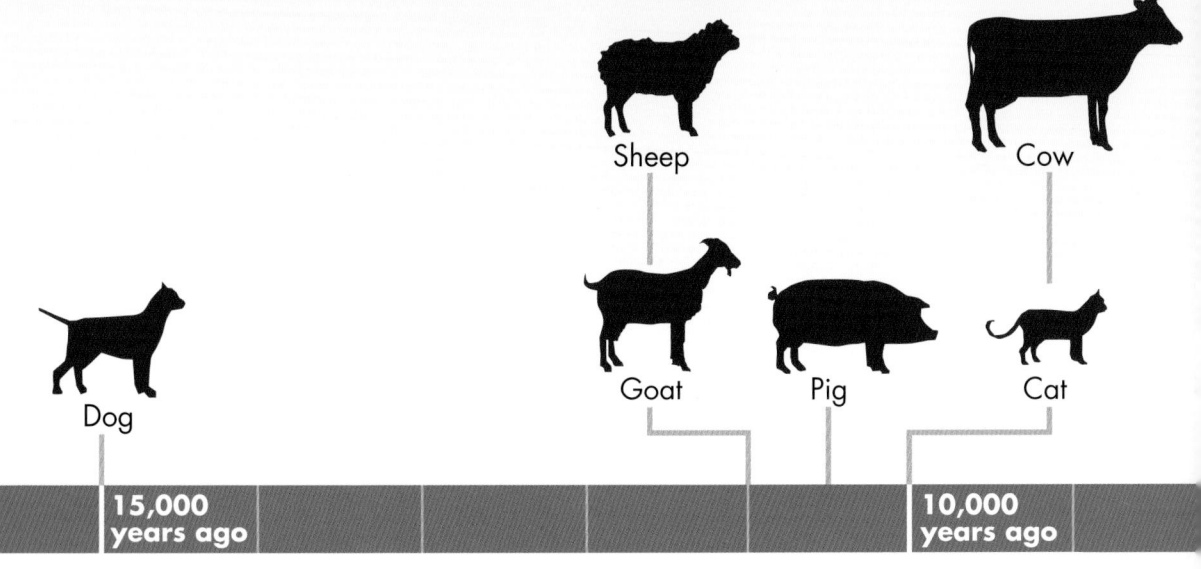

Sheep

Cow

Goat

Pig

Cat

Dog

| 15,000 years ago | | | | 10,000 years ago | |

Over a long period of time some wolves became the first dogs that lived with humans.

Other wolves continued to change a little, but lived as wild animals.

Much later, as people grew crops and lived in settled communities, they began to tame other animals that could be used for farming. The taming of wild animals to live with or beside humans is called domestication. Dogs were probably the first animals to be domesticated, followed by goats, sheep, pigs, and cattle, and then chickens and horses.

People then bred from these animals to keep the useful characteristics that were important in their work as farm animals. For example, sheep that would provide more wool, cows more milk and chickens more eggs.

This is called selective breeding.

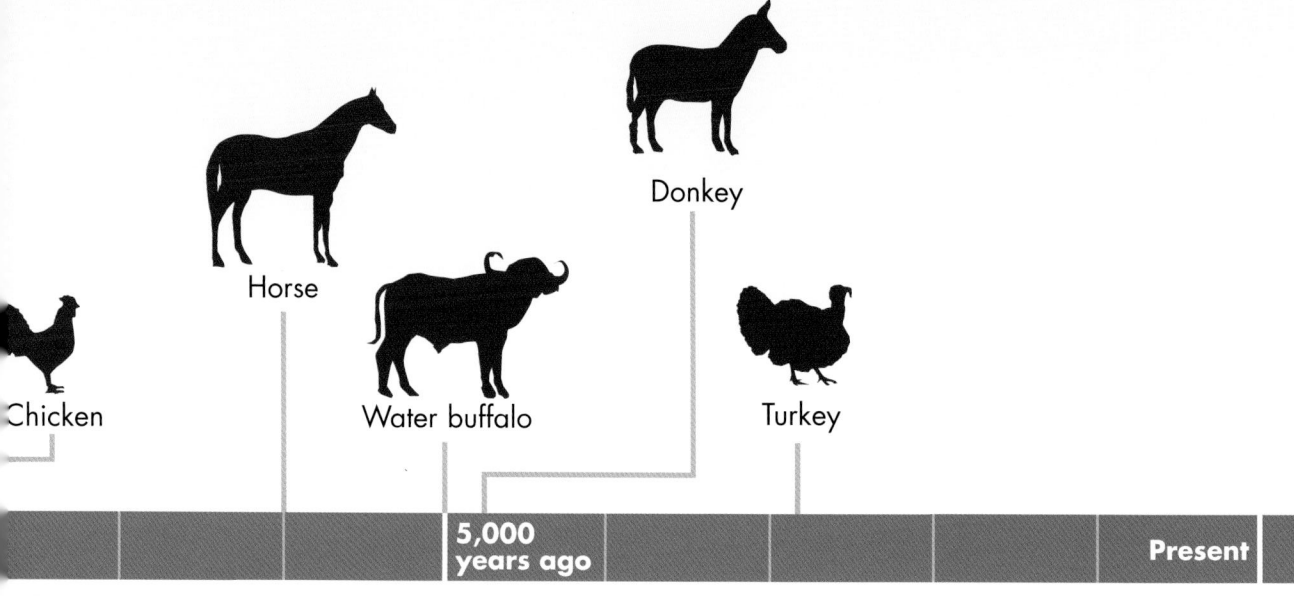

Chicken

Horse

Water buffalo

Donkey

Turkey

5,000 years ago

Present

Case study

The domestication of wolves

All current breeds of dogs and modern wolves, dingoes, foxes, coyotes, jackals and wild dogs have developed from a common ancestor. Their ancestor is the prehistoric wolf that lived in Europe and Asia.

Characteristics of wolves

Wolves are highly social animals that live in packs. A wolf pack is a small group of about eight or sometimes more animals.

• One male and one female are the pack leaders and they track and hunt prey. They choose den sites for their cubs and establish a territory or set of boundaries for their pack.
• The social bonds between members of a pack are very strong.

A pack of grey wolves

An Arctic wolf howls

Wolves spend around one third of their time travelling and searching for food. They can run great distances – 30 to 50 kilometres per day on average and up to 160 kilometres when food is scarce.

Wolves communicate through sounds – howls, whines, growls and barks. They have excellent hearing and an amazing sense of smell that they use to mark their territory and communicate with each other.

Wolves also use body language to express themselves. Facial expressions such as baring teeth and tail positions show how they feel about things around them. They use these forms of communication to show that they are in charge (dominant) or to show that they accept that another animal is in charge (subordination).

Wolves are very protective towards their pack members. They are curious, intelligent and can be highly aggressive in some situations.

Case study

The process of domestication

Developing the dogs that humans wanted began in a simple way.

Long after some wolves started to live with humans, people in Siberia used them to pull their sleds and to help them hunt larger animals. These people found that smaller dogs were better for pulling sleds because they did not overheat as quickly as larger dogs. They could work for longer hours.

Larger dogs were better for hunting as they were more powerful in dealing with bears and other large animals. Choosing pups from parents that showed special qualities such as their size or behaviour was how humans started selective breeding.

Dogs were readily able to be trained by humans because they live in packs and obey their leaders. Dogs accept some humans as the leader of their pack. People have also learned how to read a dog's body language and other communication to understand how a dog is feeling, and use this to help with their training.

Husky dogs
pulling a sled

Human needs shaped the development of dogs from wolves. By choosing particular wolf behaviours that were wanted and avoiding those behaviours that were not wanted people greatly increased the number of breeds of dogs.

Modern dogs resulted from what humans wanted to see in their dogs and how they wanted their dogs to behave.

A giant mastiff (left) and tiny chihuahua

Case study

Today, there are over 340 breeds of dogs. Over a long period of time, these main groups of dogs were developed by selective breeding.

Companion dogs

These are dogs that are kept as pets. They are expected to be loyal, sometimes playful, and give pleasure to their owners.

Working dogs

There are many kinds of working dogs.

Guide dogs help their owners who are **sight-impaired**. The ability to learn, stay calm and make good decisions together with their sharp eyesight are very important characteristics for guide dogs.

Sniffer dogs are used by police and customs officers to track missing or wanted people or to locate illegal items. Their enhanced sense of smell and their ability to be trained and to communicate with their handlers are important.

A police dog in training

Herding dogs help farmers move cattle, sheep and other animals. They need to be intelligent, obedient and have good communication skills.

Australia has its own wild dog called the dingo. It is likely that Asian people brought the dingo to Australia by boat more than 4,000 years ago. Scientists have traced its origins back to an Asian variety of the grey wolf. Most dingoes live as wild animals but some were domesticated and lived with Aboriginal people as companion dogs.

Hunting dogs

There are several types of hunting dogs. Some breeds are excellent at finding birds, making them fly or bringing them back to their owners. Excellent eyesight and being able to detect and follow a scent are essential for these dogs to help their owners.

Other breeds can find, chase and kill prey. These dogs are sometimes large, strong and aggressive, and are able to run their prey down. Small dogs are able to catch vermin that live in burrows.

Guard dogs

These dogs are large and can be trained to protect property, people, families and even animals. Most of them bark and appear aggressive and some will attack.

Conclusion

Animals have changed their bodies, their behaviours and how they have their young because the earth's environment has changed. Nearly all these changes have taken place very slowly over millions of years. Some changes are the result of humans breeding animals to suit human needs.

Animal **species compete** with each other for food, shelter and places to breed. The animals that change in ways that are best suited to their environment survive and continue to breed and develop. Those that do not are unsuccessful and eventually become **extinct**.

Glossary

ancestor the living thing that a group of living things originated from

ancient belonging to times a long time ago, in the distant past

compete to fight for the things an animal needs to survive, such as food, shelter and a place to breed

extinct when a group of living things no longer has any living members left

fossils the remains of plants or animals – or prints from living things from long, long ago – that have been preserved in rock

gene chemical information, passed on from a parent to its offspring, that controls body features

habitat the place where a plant or an animal naturally lives

molluscs a large group of animals that have a soft body and, usually, a shell but no backbone

sight-impaired a reduced ability to see that cannot be fixed with glasses or contact lenses

species a group of living things that have many traits in common and are able to have offspring

Index